HELP!
I'M DROWNING IN DEBT

HELP!
I'M DROWNING IN DEBT

dr. bill maier
general editor

ron blue
author

Tyndale House Publishers, Inc.
Carol Stream, Illinois

Editor(s): Larry Weeden, Brandy Bruce
Cover photograph © by WoodStock/Alamy. All rights reserved.

Library of Congress Cataloging-in-Publication Data
Blue, Ron, 1942-
  Help! I'm drowning in debt / by Ron Blue.
      p. cm. — (A focus on the family book)
  Rev. and updated ed. of: Taming the money monster. c1993.
  ISBN-13: 978-1-58997-455-5
  ISBN-10: 1-58997-455-7
  1. Finance, Personal. 2. Saving and investment. 3. Debt. I. Blue, Ron,
1942- Taming the money monster. II. Title.
  HG179.B5657 2007
  332.024'02—dc22

                                                     2007002995

Printed in the United States of America
1 2 3 4 5 6 7 8 9 / 13 12 11 10 09 08 07

Contents

Foreword

Are you up to your eyeballs in debt? Do you dread opening your mailbox, fearing you'll find another credit card bill or over-due notice? Do you long for the day when all of your bills will be paid and you'll have financial peace of mind? If so, this book is for you.

Author Ron Blue has been a financial planner and consultant for over 40 years. As a CPA, an MBA, and a former banker, he has helped thousands of individuals get their financial houses in order. Ron possesses a tremendous amount of insight into human nature, and he is able to quickly "hone in" on the root causes of most money problems.

This concise, well-written resource will

provide you with practical strategies to get yourself and your family out of debt. You'll learn the five immediate steps you'll need to take to get started on the road to financial security. You'll learn the four major "financial deceptions" that millions of Americans have bought into, resulting in *billions* of dollars of debt. And you'll find out why unrecognized emotional and spiritual issues may be keeping you in financial bondage.

I pray that you'll take Ron's advice to heart, and that this book will challenge and equip you to make the positive changes that will lead to financial health and spiritual contentment!

Dr. Bill Maier
Vice President, Psychologist in Residence
Focus on the Family

Introduction

Tom and Sue are a typical middle-aged, middle-class couple. There's nothing extravagant about their lifestyle, but they own a home and two cars and live comfortably. Early in their marriage, they got in the habit of buying what they wanted right away with credit cards or installment loans. As a result, they have overspent their income by just a little year after year.

Now Tom and Sue find themselves more than $7,000 in consumer debt, with no savings, no money set aside toward their children's college education, and both cars in need of replacement before long. They realize they need to change their habits before it's too late.

They're just one missed paycheck from disaster.

ๆ ๆ ๆ

Betty is a single mom with two children. Her former husband left her after running up debt on four credit cards. Because of the way our laws work, she is liable for those debts. Out of her monthly take-home pay of approximately $1,200, she gives to her church and pays rent, utilities, groceries, and so on. Her budget leaves no room for doctors, prescriptions, clothes, entertainment, or car repairs.

Like many divorced mothers, Betty receives no child support. Her former husband is over $25,000 in arrears and will probably never make that up, let alone start to make regular payments.

Betty feels the local school is too dangerous for her children, so she has placed them, at great cost, in a private school. The school has been patient with her and is helping her as much as it can, but she continues to fall further behind. She now owes $2,900 on credit cards and $1,000 to the school.

She isn't paying anything on two of the credit card balances, and she pays $35 a month on the other two. At her current rate of repayment, she will never be free of any of those debts.

As you might imagine, Betty is not too worried about the national debt, or even about what happens to tax rates. She's concerned about how to put food on the table and make next month's payments.

୨ ୨ ୨

Phil and Jenny are among the thousands of couples who started their own small business in recent years. Unfortunately, however, their efforts ended in business and personal bankruptcy (largely because of legal problems with a former partner). Although the bankruptcy freed them lawfully from the business's huge debts, they were left owing $13,000 to their lawyer and $12,000 to Jenny's parents for help received while they were still trying to keep the company afloat. The IRS also claims they owe back payroll taxes from their failed business. On top of that, Phil owes $15,000 in student loans for classes he took toward earning a master's degree in business administration.

Determined to make a fresh start, Phil and Jenny moved halfway across the country. They now have no access to credit and must pay cash for everything. Both hold down full-time jobs, but Phil still hopes to finish his master's degree. And even as they continue to repay their debts, they both dream of starting another business with growth potential so Jenny can stay home with their young children.

⁹ ⁹ ⁹

Consider your own debt situation right now. Maybe you're like Tom and Sue and you've found yourself in an ocean of debt with no solution in sight. Or maybe you can relate to Betty's situation—barely treading water and just hoping things get better.

What can you do to get your finances under control and prepare yourself for an uncertain future? The answer, which may surprise you, is that you can do quite a lot. In fact, only you can take the most important steps possible.

In this short book, we'll offer practical help on how to get out of debt and stay out of debt. (For a wider-ranging treatment of debt issues, read *Taming the*

Money Monster or see the Resources section at the back of this book for recommended materials.)

First, we'll help you start by getting a complete, realistic picture of your current financial situation. (We'll explain how to do that in detail in Part 1.) You have to know where you are before you can plan how to get where you want to be. Then we'll provide steps for reducing and even eliminating all of your debt.

We'll help you develop a healthy financial perspective, which involves exercising discipline, learning contentment, understanding true security, and realizing you can't buy personal significance.

And, finally, we'll leave you with tips on how—from this point forward—you can make good and positive financial decisions for you and your family.

Don't despair. Help is on the way!

Part
One

How to Get
Out of Debt

In the introduction, we looked at three real-life situations. Tom and Sue, who married young and continued to over-spend their income by about $500 per year, have decided they now want to get out of debt. We also looked briefly at a single mother who cannot seem to meet all her priorities without incurring more debt, and at a couple whose small business failed and saddled them with heavy debts.

In this section, we want to see specifically how those families can escape an ocean of debt and get safely to shore. In so doing, I'll explain a few basic, simple steps to getting out of debt so you can see how the process works. The steps are pretty much the same for everyone, so our approach will be to use Tom and Sue's situation as an in-depth case study. What

will work for them will also work for
Betty, for Phil and Jenny, and for you.

To put it simply: *You get out of debt
little by little over time, and the major
requirement is discipline.* The most formi-
dable aspect is that it almost always
requires a change in lifestyle and a
reordering of priorities. That's painful, and
the natural human tendency is to resist
such change. You may wish there were
some easy, painless way to get out of debt,
but no such "out" exists. If you want to be
free of a debt problem, you've got to make
up your mind, with your family's coopera-
tion, that you'll pay the price now to
enjoy financial freedom later.

The only alternatives to gradual repayment of debt are to sell assets or increase
your income. Selling assets may mean
selling a car, a boat, a house, an investment, or something else that's providing a

desired level of lifestyle now. Generating more income may mean putting a spouse to work outside the home (which I don't really recommend as a way to maintain a standard of living, as you'll see later), obtaining a second job for the breadwinner, or asking adolescent children to work part-time. Each of these alternatives requires a change in lifestyle, as something must be given up—namely, time or possessions.

Five Practical Steps to Getting Out of Debt

There are five steps to take in getting out of debt. They're easy to list, hard to do. But there's no other moral way. The five steps are:

1. Determine where you are.
2. Stop going into debt.
3. Develop a repayment plan.

4. Establish accountability.
5. Reward yourself.

Step 1: Determine Where You Are

It's interesting to hear people talk about their debt situations, because most people do not consider either a home mortgage or a car loan as debt. Those two kinds of debt have become such a standard part of our lives that we think of them differently.

The first step to getting out of debt, however, is knowing your total amount of debt. In chart 1, I've completed a listing of Tom and Sue's total debts. You'll recall that they owe more than $7,000 on five credit cards. They also have a home mortgage, but I didn't include that in this debt schedule, as that will be repaid out of their living expenses over the next 15 to 20 years.

A blank debt schedule (chart 5) is pro-

Chart 1 ■ DEBT SCHEDULE			
Lender	Amount Owed	Due Date	Payment Schedule
VISA	$3,700	Mo.	$75/Mo.
MASTERCARD	$1,900	Mo.	$85/Mo.
SEARS	$1,000	Mo.	$55/Mo.
DISCOVER	$300	Mo.	$15/Mo.
AMEX BLUE	$300	Mo.	$10/Mo.

vided at the end of Part 1 so you can list all your debts. In addition to your credit card balances, include your installment loan balances, student loan balances, mortgage balances, and any other term-note balances you owe. Then you'll have a realistic and honest appraisal of your total debt. In listing the amounts owed, do not include such regular monthly expenses as utilities, private school tuition, food, and clothing, as those are normal monthly bills and not debts.

Now that you've listed all amounts owed and you're certain of your commitments regarding debt repayments, we'll look at the next step to overcoming debt.

Step 2: Stop Going into Debt

This step is extraordinarily difficult to take, I know. It requires that you decide there will be no additional borrowing for any purpose. Before you even consider taking on more debt, you should go through the process described for evaluating the borrowing decision. (For more on this subject, see the rules for making decisions on page 80.)

If you're an overspender and in debt, however, then even the latter sections will not justify avoiding this step. You

absolutely must decide to use debt
no longer. If that requires destroying
your credit cards, my recommendation is
simple:

1. Lay your credit cards on a sheet of
   aluminum foil.
2. Put them in the oven at 450
   degrees.
3. In just a few minutes, you'll have a
   brightly colored mass of plastic.
4. After it cools, hang it in a conspicu-
   ous place to remind you of your
   decision to stop going into debt.

If you're worried about stinking up
your kitchen, you can perform "plastic
surgery" on your credit cards—using scis-
sors to cut up each card into at least eight
pieces. And if you're concerned about how
you'll get along without credit cards, let
me assure you that within just a few
months, the credit card companies will

send you new cards, unsolicited. They want you to use their cards.

Your commitment to stop using debt in any form needs to be made to another person or couple who will hold you accountable. (See Step 4 for more about this.) Hard as it is, Tom and Sue need to make this commitment.

Step 3: Develop a Repayment Plan

In addition to knowing your current debt level, you need to learn what your cash flow and your living expenses are per year. You'll notice that charts 2 and 3 on the following pages have been completed for Tom and Sue. Again, you'll find blank charts 6 and 7 at the end of Part 1 for you to complete. Note that Tom and Sue are once more planning to overspend their income by $500 unless they make changes in either their income or one of their

Chart 2 ■ LIVING EXPENSE SUMMARY

	Amount Paid Monthly	Other Than Monthly	Total Annual Amount
Housing:			
Mortgage/Rent	875		
Insurance			
Property Taxes			
Electricity	120		
Heating	40		
Water	25		
Sanitation	20		
Telephone	75		
Cleaning			
Repairs/Maintenance			
Supplies			
Other			
Total Housing	1,155		13,860
Food Total	400		4,800
Clothing Total		1,000	1,000
Transportation:			
Insurance		500	
Gas and Oil	150		
Repairs/Maintenance			
Parking			
Other			

Chart 2 ■ LIVING EXPENSE SUMMARY *(cont.)*			
	Amount Paid Monthly	Other Than Monthly	Total Annual Amount
Total Transportation	150	500	2,300
Entertainment/Recreation:			
Eating Out	25		
Baby-sitters			
Magazines/Newspapers		50	
Vacation		500	
Clubs/Activities			
Other			
Total Enter./Rec.	25	550	850
Medical Expenses:			
Insurance			
Doctors	50		
Dentist	25		
Drugs	25		
Other			
Total Medical	100		1,200
Insurance:			
Life		200	
Disability			
Other			
Total Insurance		200	200
Children:			

Chart 2 ■ LIVING EXPENSE SUMMARY (cont.)			
	Amount Paid Monthly	Other Than Monthly	Total Annual Amount
School Lunches			
Allowances	40		
Tuition			
Lessons	60		
Other			
Total Children	100		1,200
Gifts:			
Christmas		300	
Birthdays		200	
Anniversary		100	
Other			
Total Gifts		600	600
Miscellaneous:			
Toiletries	25		
Husband: misc.	50		
Wife: misc.	50		
Cleaning/Laundry			
Animal Care	25		
Beauty/Barber	15		
Other	100		
Total Miscellaneous	265		3,180
TOTAL EXPENSES	2,195	2,850	29,190

Chart 3 ■ CASH FLOW SUMMARY	
Gross Income:	$ 35,000
Less:	
Giving	(1,200)
Taxes (from pay stubs)	(2,230)
Debt Payments (from chart 1)	(2,880)
Living Expenses (from chart 2)	(29,190)
Cash Flow Margin:	$< 500 >

spending areas (for example, giving, taxes, living expenses, or debt repayments).

If you've never before tallied your living expenses in such a manner, go to an office supply store and buy a simple ledger book. (You can also do this in a spreadsheet program on your computer, if you prefer.) It should have at least 31 vertical columns (one for each day of the month) on each two-page spread. List the expense categories down the left-hand side of the spread, and for one month, record each day's expenses in each category in the column for that day.

At the end of the month, total the expenses in each category on the right-hand side of the spread. For non-monthly expenses (for example, life insurance), review your checkbook register and other financial records from the past year.

You should now know where you are in terms of debt, cash flow, and living expenses. Having also made the commitment to stop going into debt, you can develop a strategy for repaying those debts. There is no one "right way" of repaying your obligations. Several suggestions follow, any one of which (or a combination) might work in your particular situation.

Sell Assets. The first idea for repaying your debts is to determine if you have any assets that can be sold. Even small things that could be sold through a garage sale—clothes that aren't worn anymore, sports equipment that's no longer used, books already read—can help you get out of smaller debts. (Like most couples, Tom and Sue have a lot of things gathering dust that could go into a garage sale.)

The sale of bigger items such as cars, investments, and perhaps even homes should also be considered. As I said earlier, that may require a change in lifestyle, but how badly do you want to be free from the bondage of debt?

Use Savings Accounts. You should consider using savings accounts or surplus cash balances in checking accounts to pay off debts. Using a low-yielding savings account to pay off high-cost debt is a guaranteed high-yield investment. If you have a savings account and are still carrying credit card or installment debt, consider using those funds from your savings account to reduce debt. (Note, though, that you should keep at least one month of living expenses in an easily accessible account as an emergency fund, and you should *not* use that money to pay off debt.)

If you take this approach, replenish your savings accounts as soon as the debt is paid off. Just keep paying the same amount you had been putting toward credit cards and installment debt into your savings.

Double Payments. A third strategy for getting out of debt is to double up on your payments. I recently received a letter from someone who indicated he paid $60 per month on one credit card, thinking he was reducing the debt. In fact, however, he was paying only a few dollars on principal each month and making no real dent in the total owed. But by doubling up on the payments and cutting expenses in another area of the budget, it's possible to pay off debt much more quickly.

Keep Payments Constant. A fourth strategy is relatively painless but nonetheless essential: Keep constant the total amount of payments you're making each month. Concentrate on paying off your smallest debt first. That's the quickest way to be rid of one debt, and it will encourage you to keep going. When that debt is gone, rather than spending the amount freed up by no longer having that payment, apply it to the next-smallest debt (in addition to what you were already paying on that debt). It's like climbing a ladder, beginning at the bottom and working your way to the top.

For example, if you have several credit

card and installment payments totaling $500 per month, instead of reducing the amount paid each month as the debts are eliminated, continue to send a total of $500 per month, always increasing the payments to the smallest debt first. As you move up the ladder of debt, the obligations are paid off that much more rapidly.

In the case of Tom and Sue, they are now paying a total of $240 per month on their credit card bills (see chart 1). Using this strategy, they might make minimum payments on the larger balances such as those for Visa, MasterCard, and Sears. Then they could take the rest of what they had been paying to those accounts and apply it, first of all, to their American Express Blue credit card bill, which would probably be paid off in one month.

Next, by keeping their payments constant at $240, still maintaining minimum payments to the larger account balances, they could apply all the excess to Discover until it's paid off. Then they could tackle the Sears bill with the same strategy.

Within six months, three of the five credit cards would be paid off. Within 12 months, four of the five would be clear. By the second year, they would be paying off only one card balance: $240 a month to Visa. They may still need 12 to 24 months to eliminate that debt because of the accumulating interest, but it's easier emotionally to have just one credit card to deal with instead of receiving five bills every month.

Reduce Living Expenses. A fifth strategy is to review your living expense summary (chart 5) and, as a family, decide where you can cut expenses. Apply the amount cut to specific debts. You might decide to cut down on your entertainment, clothing, food (especially eating out), or home-maintenance budgets—whatever fits your family situation. The fact is that in almost every family budget, as much as 10 to 20 percent could be used to repay debt. Again, it will require a change in lifestyle, but that cost will be more than offset by the sense of satisfaction in seeing yourself gradually get free of payments.

Reduce Tax Withholdings. A sixth strategy is available if you're now receiving a federal income tax refund each year: Reduce your tax withholdings, and apply the increase in take-home pay to your debt repayment. The IRS does not require you to pay in withholdings (or estimated payments) any more than what you will actually owe. It's a simple matter to decrease your withholding to the amount of the actual projected liability.

Here's how to reduce your withholdings: First, determine your tax liability for the year. Begin by looking at last year's federal income tax return to see how much you paid. Then calculate the effect of any relevant changes this year (a raise, the birth of a child, having an older child become self-supporting, etc.). You can do this by going to the IRS Web site (www.irs.gov) and searching for the "IRS Withholding Calculator," which will guide you step-by-step through the process of determining what your tax liability for the year is going to be.

After you have determined what you're likely to owe in federal taxes, you can have your withholdings decreased to no more than that amount. Simply go to your company's personnel office and fill out a new W-4 form. Employers are required in some cases to report significant changes in withholding requests to the IRS, but that's no problem if you're using an actual tax projection.

The fact is that a regular tax refund is a sign of poor financial management. You're allowing the government to use your money interest-free, whereas you could be using that same money to pay off high-interest debt.

In the cases of Tom and Sue and Betty (the single mom), if either state or federal income taxes are being withheld from their paychecks, it's possible their withholdings could be reduced. This is certainly an area they need to look into as a way of increasing their disposable income.

Consider Counseling. In severe debt situations, the repayment plan may require professional assistance. There's nothing disgraceful about asking for help. You might be a single mother (like Betty) with several children to support, for example, and increasing your income, selling assets, or decreasing expenses aren't viable alternatives.

The help you need might be found at a local credit counseling agency. (See the Resources section for further help.)

There may be other strategies you could use, and the ones offered here are only suggestions. The important thing is that you develop your own strategy and then implement it. In making your plans for debt reduction, however, there are

certain things you absolutely should
not do.

੭ ੭ ੭

Do Not Decrease Giving. The first is that if
you are actively giving to a place of wor-
ship, you shouldn't decrease your giving.
For people of faith, giving should be the
first-priority use of money, because it's a
recognition of God's ownership of everything you have.

The only time when a reduction in
giving to repay debt might be acceptable
is if the debt situation is extremely severe,
you have prepared a budget that cuts out
all surplus uses of money, and the decision to decrease giving is only temporary.
In those circumstances, giving may be
temporarily decreased. This would be a
good idea for Betty, the single mom who

will never get out of debt without taking
some such action.

Do Not Use Tax Money. Second, do not
reduce your tax payments *below* your
projected liability. If you do, you're just borrowing from the government to pay someone else. You aren't really reducing your
debt at all. The day of reckoning is merely
postponed to the following April 15.

Do Not Use a Debt Consolidation Loan.
Third, in most cases you should not take
out a debt consolidation loan. The typical
reason for such a loan is that it "feels
good," but it doesn't solve the basic problem. Many people who go for debt consolidation find they have to come back to
it frequently because they have not really
solved their spending problems.

If you're seeing a debt counselor, however, and the counselor recommends a
debt consolidation loan as your only

alternative—and if the counselor will work with you to set up a realistic budget—then it may be appropriate. But it should be a one-time solution.

Do Not Add a Second Full-time Income. The last recommendation regarding what not to do is the one violated most often by couples. Namely, if the wife is currently a homemaker, she should not get a job to increase the family's income. When you consider the additional expenses of giving, taxes, child care, transportation, wardrobe, and so on associated with the second job, the economic benefit of a second income is almost nonexistent.

Besides, most debt problems are spending problems, not income problems. If a homemaker goes to work to fund a consumptive lifestyle, the root problems have not been identified and eliminated.

I realize there are exceptions to this

general rule: A family may face unexpected medical bills, or parents may desire to send their children to a private school for good reasons. But given human nature, extra income tends only to raise the level of discontent, increasing the desire for more and more "things" that won't meet real needs.

Step 4: Establish Accountability

I've found that people generally benefit from accountability. If you must report to someone you respect on a commitment you've made voluntarily, such as getting out of debt, you're more likely to follow through. If you're unwilling, however, to verbalize to another person your commitment to get out of debt, be it to your spouse or, preferably, another person, the likelihood of your following through is reduced dramatically.

In Tom and Sue's case, they have made their commitment to each other, and they're pretty good at helping one another toe the line. They've also discussed their decision to escape their ocean of debt with their parents and several friends.

Ask someone to hold you accountable, not in a general sense, but specifically to make certain payments on designated dates. Set up a schedule of reporting times. Establish the length of the accountability period. In other words, neither the commitment nor the time is open-ended.

When you ask that person or couple to hold you accountable, be honest about why you're doing it. Most people who care about you would be honored to help.

Step 5: Reward Yourself

When we have something positive to look forward to, we're encouraged to maintain the disciplines required to get there. Many people who have trouble losing weight, for example, develop a reward system that motivates them to maintain a diet. In the same manner, it's a good idea to reward yourself as you pay off debt.

When you pay off your first debt, for instance, you might treat yourself to a special lunch. When the second debt is paid off, you could enjoy a nice dinner. When the third debt is paid off, it might be time for a more expensive treat like a weekend away. Paying off the fourth or final debt could result in a reward such as clothes or furniture.

Obviously, you don't want to get yourself into more debt through your reward system. The idea is to find ways to motivate yourself to maintain the disciplines required to get out of debt. They don't have to cost much money—or any at all.

You might look forward, for example, to a coupon-book-burning ceremony or to hanging a homemade "Graduation from Debt" certificate on the family-room wall. Whatever the rewards you choose, they need to be personally motivational. The most significant reward will be the financial freedom that comes from getting out of debt.

Getting Started

The steps I've outlined are all that's required to be relieved of the bondage of debt. The key is to take the first step. Someone once asked, "How do you eat an elephant?" The answer is, "One bite at a time." Getting out of debt is likewise done one step at a time. It may appear to be an impossible task at this point, but I'm convinced that you can do it, just as many before you have.

Since getting started is usually the most difficult part of any task, chart 8 (on page 44) is for you to use to begin the process of swimming out of your personal ocean of debt. You can refer to chart 4 on the following page to see Tom and Sue's action plan. Complete the chart prayerfully and promptly. Now is the best time to begin.

Chart 4 ■ ACTION PLAN		
Step	**Action**	**Completion Date**
1. Determine where you are.	1. Complete chart 2	1. done
	2. Complete chart 3	2. done
	3.	3.
	4.	4.
2. Stop going into debt.	1. Destroy credit cards.	1. done
	2. Use cash only.	2.
	3.	3.
	4.	4.
3. Develop repayment plan.	1. Yard sale, pay AMEX.	1.
	2. Sell TV, pay Discover.	2.
	3. $220/mo. to Sears.	3.
	4.	4.
4. Establish accountability.	1. Pray for right person.	1. immediately
	2. Ask him/her.	2.
	3. Set date for meeting.	3.
	4. Set meeting schedule.	4.
5. Reward yourself.	1. Dinner at Mac's.	1. AMEX paid off
	2.	2.
	3.	3.

Chart 5 ■ DEBT SCHEDULE			
Lender	**Amount Owed**	**Due Date**	**Payment Schedule**

Chart 6 ■ LIVING EXPENSE SUMMARY			
	Amount Paid Monthly	Other Than Monthly	Total Annual Amount
Housing:			
Mortgage/Rent			
Insurance			
Property Taxes			
Electricity			
Heating			
Water			
Sanitation			
Telephone			
Cleaning			
Repairs/Maintenance			
Supplies			
Other			
Total Housing			
Food Total			
Clothing Total			
Transportation:			
Insurance			
Gas and Oil			
Repairs/Maintenance			
Parking			
Other			

Chart 6 ■ LIVING EXPENSE SUMMARY (cont.)

	Amount Paid Monthly	Other Than Monthly	Total Annual Amount
Total Transportation			
Entertainment/Recreation:			
Eating Out			
Baby-sitters			
Magazines/Newspapers			
Vacation			
Clubs/Activities			
Other			
Total Enter./Rec.			
Medical Expenses:			
Insurance			
Doctors			
Dentist			
Drugs			
Other			
Total Medical			
Insurance:			
Life			
Disability			
Other			
Total Insurance			
Children:			

Chart 6 ■ LIVING EXPENSE SUMMARY *(cont.)*			
	Amount Paid Monthly	Other Than Monthly	Total Annual Amount
School Lunches			
Allowances			
Tuition			
Lessons			
Other			
Total Children			
Gifts:			
Christmas			
Birthdays			
Anniversary			
Other			
Total Gifts			
Miscellaneous:			
Toiletries			
Husband: misc.			
Wife: misc.			
Cleaning/Laundry			
Animal Care			
Beauty/Barber			
Other			
Total Miscellaneous			
TOTAL EXPENSES			

Chart 7 ■ CASH FLOW SUMMARY	
Gross Income:	$
Less:	
Giving	( )
Taxes	( )
Debt Payments (from chart 5)	( )
Living Expenses (from chart 6)	( )
Cash Flow Margin:	$

Chart 8 ■ ACTION PLAN		
Step	**Action**	**Completion Date**
1. Determine where you are.	1.	1.
	2.	2.
	3.	3.
2. Stop going into debt.	1.	1.
	2.	2.
	3.	3.
3. Develop repayment plan.	1.	1.
	2.	2.
	3.	3.
4. Establish accountability.	1.	1.
	2.	2.
	3.	3.
5. Reward yourself.	1.	1.
	2.	2.

How to Keep
from Getting
Back into
Debt

Tom and Sue are now aware of how to get out of debt and are committed to doing so. But they're concerned that they might slip back into debt if they're not careful. How can they prevent that? What else do they need to learn?

Besides staying out of debt, Tom and Sue's biggest current financial concern is their two cars. Both are more than 10 years old and in need of major repairs. Fortunately, both cars are still drivable and safe.

Tom and Sue wonder if it's worthwhile to make the repairs, because even if they're made, the cars will still need to be replaced eventually. They also don't have the $1,200 needed to make the repairs, but neither do they have the money to replace the cars. Until now, their response would have been to put the repairs on their credit cards once again and hope that before too long—with new car loans—they could replace the cars.

Sally, one of their daughters (they have two), needs braces, too (about $3,500). The orthodontist would let Tom and Sue pay them off at $100 per month.

Their monthly budget is tight; their single largest expense is a house payment of $875. They still don't save anything and don't see how they can. Their question is, "How do we manage all our expenses and still stay out of debt?"

My advice is simple but not simplistic: First, when unavoidable costs come up—like car repairs—Tom and Sue should study their budget and look for areas where they could cut back temporarily on other expenses (such as clothing, eating out, etc.). Maintaining a budget is key to successfully monitoring spending and managing expenses.

Second, they need to understand and avoid the common deceptions that often lead people into debt.

More deception (most of it unintended) is perpetrated by accountants, bankers, business schools, and business-people regarding the use of debt than most of us realize. We tend to respect these professionals. Yet they only pass on what they've been taught, and in many cases they've been taught half-truths. And people like Tom and Sue have bought into them.

Being a CPA, a former banker, an alumnus of a graduate business school, and a businessman myself, I remember what I was taught and have in turn taught others in times past. There are four major financial deceptions conveyed implicitly or explicitly by my peer groups. They are as follows:

1. Borrowed money is always paid back with cheaper dollars in the future.
2. The tax deductibility of interest makes using debt a wise thing to do.
3. Inflation is inevitable; therefore, it is always wise to buy now at a lower cost than in the future at a higher price.
4. Leverage (debt) is magic.

Perhaps I'm too critical to call these deceptions, because they may or may not be true depending on certain assumptions. But the assumptions underlying the four statements are not adequately explained. So to better understand the whole issue of using debt wisely (if, in fact, you should use it at all), you must recognize these deceptions and be able to evaluate them relative to your own circumstances. Otherwise, even after climbing out of your ocean of debt, you're likely to find your-self diving right back in.

Common Financial Deceptions

Deception 1: Paying Back Borrowed Money with Cheaper Dollars
In times of severe inflation, you'll hear lots of people—including "experts"—saying that prices are going to keep climbing indefinitely. The "wisdom" that goes along with this perspective is that you will always be able to pay back borrowed money with dollars that are worth less in the future, because inflation eats away at the purchasing power of money. (The dollar that is used to buy two candy bars may soon be enough only for one. And I remember when they were only a nickel!)

This wisdom is true as long as two basic assumptions are met. The first is that you're able to borrow at a fixed interest rate so your rate does not increase with inflation. The second is that inflation will, in fact, continue.

The example used most frequently to sell this deception is the purchase of a home using a fixed-rate, long-term mortgage. This does in fact make sense in a time of inflation, because the dollars used to pay back the principal amount borrowed are worth less and less. In addition, when the interest rate is fixed for the life of the loan, you can't be hurt by the increasing interest rates that go hand in hand with inflation. That logic holds if the two assumptions continue to be valid. (And if you're going to borrow to buy a house, a fixed-rate mortgage is *always* the safest kind of loan.)

History proves, however, that there are economic cycles. In other words, prices sometimes go *down*, too. This may not be geographically universal, but it does occur.

According to an article in *Money* magazine, when Debbie Daly and her husband realized home prices in their area had doubled in the four years since they'd bought their home in Calabasas, California, they were both excited and anxious, for good reason: "The 37-year-old mom had been a real estate agent in the early- to mid-1990s, when home prices in Southern California fell 40%. 'I remember what that was like,' she recalls. 'I sat around the kitchen table with people who couldn't pay off their mortgage with proceeds from their house sale.'"[1]

Other illustrations abound. The point is that even if inflation were a valid assumption overall, it may not be valid for the region in which you live. When industries leave an area, inflation changes. There aren't as many people demanding the same goods and services, so prices tend to fall. Thus, what is true today regarding inflation may not be true tomorrow.

This uncertainty about the future direction of prices and interest rates is what makes a fixed-rate mortgage safer than an adjustable-rate mortgage (ARM). But the notion that you can "beat the system" by borrowing at a fixed rate is naive. It assumes that lenders don't really know their business, when in fact they know exactly what they're doing.

First, during periods of inflation, lenders raise interest rates. Second, they promote mortgages that protect them against further inflation, like adjustable-rate and interest-only loans. (With an ARM, if interest rates rise, so will the rate on your mortgage, as often as the loan agreement allows—and with it the size of your monthly payment.)

Third, lenders know, too, that the average home loan will mature (be paid off) within just 8 years, not 30, as borrowers sell or refinance. Then the money from the payoff of that mortgage can be reloaned on the same house at a higher interest rate.

Additionally, every time lenders make loans, they can charge points and fees that increase their income. Thus, they don't make bad decisions even when they're willing to make fixed-rate loans. Lenders push as much of the risk to the borrower as they possibly can. And in times of inflation, they charge premium rates.

Whenever you borrow money at a premium interest rate, the fact of paying back with cheaper dollars in the future is mitigated by the high rate of interest. In my 40 years of professional experience, interest rates on credit card and installment debt have never been lower than the inflation rate except for very short periods. So while you may repay the loan with cheaper dollars, the premium interest rates charged more than offset the benefit.

Deception 2: The Tax Deductibility of Interest

Don't be deceived that because interest is tax deductible, it's a good idea to have interest expense in order to reduce income taxes. There's a certain amount of truth to that, but it doesn't present the whole picture. First, not all interest is 100 percent tax deductible. Consumer interest (credit cards, car loans, installment loans) isn't, and even investment interest has limitations. The only 100 percent deductible interest is home mortgage interest, and that has limits, too, when the mortgage goes above a certain amount.

Second, to say that an amount is deductible only means that it's deducted from income before computing the taxes owed. It doesn't mean that taxes are offset dollar for dollar by the amount of interest.

For example, if you pay a total of 30 percent in state and federal income taxes, then for every dollar of fully deductible interest you pay, you reduce your taxes by $.30, not $1.00. Thus, the net cost of paying interest is $.70 rather than $1.00, but it's still a net cost. To say that interest is tax deductible and therefore a good idea actually means it may offer a partial benefit.

To clarify whether you should borrow based on the fact that interest offers a tax deduction, I propose this agreement: If you'll lend me $1,000, I promise to never repay you. That way you can deduct the $1,000 as a bad debt expense and reduce your taxes accordingly. I, on the other hand, will keep the $1,000, report it as income, and pay the taxes. You tell me which of us will be better off. Interest deductions operate the same way.

Deception 3: It Will Cost More Later

As I mentioned earlier, whenever inflation rates are relatively high, a common advertising theme is "Buy now, because it will cost more later." In fact, things *will* cost more later. However, that ploy begs the true question, which is not "What will it cost later?" but "Do I really need it?"

The second aspect of this deception is the underlying assumption that everything will continue to go up in price. That's not always the case. Personal computer prices, for example, tend to start high when a new model is introduced and then fall steadily. And almost everything goes on sale periodically.

The way to understand the real question when tempted by this deception is to ask, "So what?" In most cases, the answer to that question is, "I may not need it later," or "The future price makes no difference to me, because I have to have it." But making a purchase on the basis of it costing more later is a short-term perspective and may well be a financial mistake.

Deception 4: The Magic of Leverage

In graduate school, I was taught the value of OPM—the use of other people's money. The idea is that if you use debt to purchase something, you get a far greater return on your portion of the investment than you would if you paid cash for it.

The classic example is, again, the purchase of a home. If you were to purchase a $160,000 home and put 10 percent down, you would have invested $16,000 of your own money. If that home then appreciated 10 percent in one year (meaning you could sell the house for $176,000), you would have a 100 percent return on the money you invested (a $16,000 gain on an $16,000 investment).

If, on the other hand, you paid cash for the home, you would have achieved only a 10 percent return (a $16,000 gain on an $160,000 investment). The difference between a 100 percent return and a 10 percent return is the magic of leverage.

During inflationary times, "sophisticated" people expand the concept to say that it's always unwise to use your own money and always wise to borrow as much as you possibly can for whatever purpose.

Those who don't understand the risks and assumptions buy into the idea.

This concept will work as illustrated if the underlying assumptions hold true. The basic assumption is that there will always be appreciation rather than depreciation on whatever is purchased—an idea I've already shown to be false.

The second assumption is that if you borrow money instead of paying cash, you have an alternative use for the money that will yield a return greater than your cost. Borrowing to buy a car at 12 percent interest, for instance, assumes that you can earn more than 12 percent by investing your money. But the only way you can earn that kind of return is to put your money in risky investments.

Many people have gone bankrupt trying to take advantage of leverage. They didn't understand the real assumptions they were making. Even huge lending institutions all over this country have gone bankrupt because they lacked this understanding.

Leverage can work for you, but it's like riding an alligator: It's a lot easier to get on than it is to get off safely.

ｏ ｏ ｏ

The best way to conclude this section is to advise you that if a deal sounds too good to be true, it probably is. Second, be very careful when accepting counsel from anyone, including supposedly knowledge-able business and professional people. Truly successful people don't become well-off by using complex techniques or even by reducing their taxes to nothing. Instead, they become successful the old-fashioned way: They earn it.

The key to financial success is to spend less than you earn and do it for a long time. That's a basic truth of money management that will never change. There are no shortcuts to escaping an ocean of debt.

Part Three

Developing a Healthy Perspective Toward Debt

According to an article in *Money* magazine, "Michael and Cynthia Proctor never asked for their first credit cards. Four of them more or less appeared pre-approved in the couple's Huntsville, Texas mailbox. . . . At the time, Michael, now 35, and Cynthia, 34, together made $43,000 working for the Texas Department of Corrections. Michael was also studying nights for his master's degree in criminology. But for all [this] schooling, the Proctors had never learned to control debt. . . .

"'We used credit cards for everything,' recalls Cynthia. . . . The Proctors were especially nonchalant about drawing cash advances. . . . Still . . . they easily made the minimum payments, and when they reached the limit on one card, they just got another.

"[Within three years,] they owed

$34,500 . . . on some 60 open credit-card accounts. Most payments were at least six weeks behind. Dunning letters from creditors arrived almost daily. . . . Stress was tearing the family apart."[2]

An article in *USA Today* tells us the story of Tim and Caren Mayberry:

"Tim earns more than $100,000 a year as a senior bank loan officer; Caren makes about $65,000 a year as a physical therapist. Yet despite their ample salaries, they say they're 'absolutely unable to put money aside, except with retirement accounts.'. . .

"A heavy debt load stands in the way of putting away more retirement money. The couple owes $285,000 on their mortgage . . . plus about $125,000 in other debt, including on credit cards and loans to buy a car, a motorcycle and a boat."[3]

The Proctors' and Mayberrys' plights illustrate how the misuse of credit can put a family not only under a lot of stress but even into bondage. I'm concerned that trouble with debt is always and only a symptom of something else. Thus, if you're going to remedy a debt problem, it's essential to understand how and why you got into debt in the first place. Or, to put it another way, you need to develop a healthy perspective on debt.

The Road to Debt

There are four common causes of problem debt. They're somewhat overlapping, and they're shared by all kinds of people, regardless of race, religion, social status, and so on. In other words, you may see yourself in more than one category. The causes are:

1. A lack of discipline.
2. A lack of contentment.
3. A search for security.
4. A search for significance.

Lack of Discipline

Based on my professional experience, I've concluded that most people who find themselves drowning in consumer debt are there because of a lack of self-discipline.

To illustrate the consequences, assume the following: A hypothetical husband and wife have a combined first-year salary of $40,000 that increases by $1,000 per year. They overspend their income by $1,000 per year, and they pay only the interest on their growing debt each year. The interest rate they pay is 10 percent. Chart 9 shows what happens to them over a period of time.

First, what began as a small problem— $100 per year for debt repayments on an income of $40,000—grows over time to $2,000 per year committed to debt repayment. The $2,000 represents 3.39 percent of their total income that is precommitted

Chart 9 ■ DEBT GROWTH					
Yr.	Income	Expense	Difference	Total Debt	Total Payment	Payment as % of Income
1	$40,000	$41,000	($1,000)	$1,000	$100	0.25%
2	41,000	42,000	($1,000)	2,000	200	0.49
3	42,000	43,000	($1,000)	3,000	300	0.71
4	43,000	44,000	($1,000)	4,000	400	0.93
5	44,000	45,000	($1,000)	5,000	500	1.14
6	45,000	46,000	($1,000)	6,000	600	1.33
7	46,000	47,000	($1,000)	7,000	700	1.52
8	47,000	48,000	($1,000)	8,000	800	1.70
9	48,000	49,000	($1,000)	9,000	900	1.88
10	49,000	50,000	($1,000)	10,000	1,000	2.04
11	50,000	51,000	($1,000)	11,000	1,100	2.20
12	51,000	52,000	($1,000)	12,000	1,200	2.35
13	52,000	53,000	($1,000)	13,000	1,300	2.50
14	53,000	54,000	($1,000)	14,000	1,400	2.64
15	54,000	55,000	($1,000)	15,000	1,500	2.78
16	55,000	56,000	($1,000)	16,000	1,600	2.91
17	56,000	57,000	($1,000)	17,000	1,700	3.04
18	57,000	58,000	($1,000)	18,000	1,800	3.16
19	58,000	59,000	($1,000)	19,000	1,900	3.28
20	59,000	60,000	($1,000)	20,000	2,000	3.39

Chart 10 ■ DEBT REPAYMENT					
Yr.	Income	Expense	Difference	Total Debt	Total Payment	Payment as % of Income
21	$60,000	$56,200	$3,800	$18,000	$3,800	6.33%
22	61,000	57,400	3,600	16,000	3,600	5.90
23	62,000	58,600	3,400	14,000	3,400	5.48
24	63,000	59,800	3,200	12,000	3,200	5.08
25	64,000	61,000	3,000	10,000	3,000	4.69
26	65,000	62,200	2,800	8,000	2,800	4.31
27	66,000	63,400	2,600	6,000	2,600	3.94
28	67,000	64,600	2,400	4,000	2,400	3.58
29	68,000	65,800	2,200	2,000	2,200	3.24
30	69,000	67,000	2,000	0	2,000	2.90

and can't be used for any other purpose.

Second, because it's taken 20 years to reach this point, the couple may have been unaware of their compounding debt problem. Without understanding why, they've probably been experiencing increasing financial frustration as debt repayment takes an ever-increasing percentage of their income.

Third, after 20 years of marriage, this man and woman have one or more children at or near college age. But just as they're approaching the highest financial-need years, they have a decreasing amount of money available to meet those needs. It's easy to see why their lack of self-discipline over a long period might now cause frustration, confusion, conflict, and anger. A small problem has grown into a huge headache.

If these people now decide they want to begin repaying their debt over 10 years, or $2,000 per year plus interest, they will experience in years 21 to 30 what chart 10 outlines. To make that payment in year 21, their total expenses must go down by $3,800 from the previous year, even though they received a $1,000 raise. Debt repayment as a percentage of their total income almost doubles. Note further that it takes four years before they reach the same level of spending they had prior to choosing to get out of debt.

In other words, the choice to start repaying debt means stepping back in their spending to the level at which they had been four years previously. It's no wonder many people throw in the towel at this point and say, "It's not worth the cost to get out of debt!"

As bad as this couple's situation looks, it's actually unusual to see people who have a self-discipline problem overspending by only $1,000 per year. That's a minimal level of overspending. My experience is that most people who lack discipline don't even realize they're overspending, because the one thing that will cure the problem—a budget—is anathema to them.

This hypothetical case also understates a problem in that most consumer debt costs a lot more than 10 percent interest; it's more likely to be 18 or even 21 percent. The example ignores the costs of taxes and charitable giving, too.

If the couple receives a $1,000 raise per year and pays in taxes and giving a total of 30 percent, they have only $700 per year in additional spendable income. When receiving a raise, however, most people assume they have the full amount to spend. If they therefore increase their spending by $1,000 per year, they're going into an even deeper hole than what's illustrated.

Being self-disciplined means making the right decisions consistently. Some people are just naturally more self-disciplined than others because of their personalities, and some have learned self-discipline over time. Because of what self-discipline is, how it's learned, and how it's applied on a daily basis, there are many ways to acquire it. This book may aid you in the process, but the ultimate solution is up to you.

Lack of Contentment

A lack of discipline may be caused by a lack of contentment. The problem could be stated this way: *If I lived someplace else, had something else, or did something else, I would be content*. But contentment is really a choice.

Many things cause discontent. Reading and believing ads is a common cause. Another is browsing in shopping malls, which can raise your level of discontent to the point that it becomes almost impossible not to yield to the temptation to buy. It's the same as putting a drink in front of an alcoholic. Not surprisingly, the level of personal debt and the amount of time people spend in front of television and in shopping malls have both increased dramatically in the last 30 years.

Contentment is found by understanding and accepting a few important truths: More lasting joy is found by nurturing relationships with friends and loved ones than by buying things. It is much healthier to focus on what we *have* than on what we *don't*. Contentment is also a spiritual issue. Replacing an "I want" attitude with an "I'm grateful for what I have" attitude begins in the heart.

Search for Security

A couple in the Northeast inherited a large sum of money a few years ago. The wife spent almost the entire inheritance buying and then decorating a new home. She was searching desperately for the security of a home that she never experienced as a child. Having almost depleted their small fortune, the couple seemed to think that borrowing was the only way they could maintain their lifestyle.

Men often evidence a search for security by their desire to participate in get-rich-quick schemes. I've seen many people compromise their standards and good judgment to try to quickly achieve the "financial independence" they think will make them secure. But being able to earn even hundreds of thousands of dollars a year by exploiting others will never provide ultimate security.

Search for Significance

The drive for significance is another reason people make foolish financial decisions. In my observation, this is more of a male problem than a female problem.

As a man, I can readily identify with

the drive for significance. Unfortunately, men often attempt to achieve significance through investments, businesses, possessions, and sexual conquests. They also try to meet this need through heavy borrowing, which threatens the security of their wives. As has been said, "The only difference between men and boys is the price of their toys."

After I spoke to a group of clients on one occasion, a former client who had been invited to the dinner approached me. He asked if I knew anyone who could lend him some money, because he was on the verge of bankruptcy. This was quite a turnaround for him, since he had retired financially secure from a large corporation.

Following retirement, he had started a new business both to occupy his time and to give him an ongoing sense of worth. The business had done well, which encouraged him to speculate in undeveloped land and other real-estate investments using large amounts of borrowed money. Then the economy in his area turned down, and his real-estate deals soured. His drive for significance through investments destroyed his previously secure financial position.

Both security and significance are legitimate needs. Likewise, the problems of lack of discipline, of contentment, of security, and of significance are timeless. They just happen to manifest themselves in our culture through getting into debt because of the ease of borrowing.

Four Rules for Making Borrowing Decisions

So, as part of your healthy new perspective on debt, how and when is it okay to

borrow? Let's look at four rules to follow
in making every such decision.

I use these rules in making my own
borrowing decisions, and I recommend
them to you in making yours:

Rule 1: Common sense
Rule 2: A guaranteed way to repay
Rule 3: Peace of heart and mind
Rule 4: Unity

These rules don't necessarily make it
easy to decide about taking on debt. The
reason we even consider going into debt
is to meet a need or a desire that has
become a high priority for us. In many
cases, however, the temptation to use
credit to meet the perceived need over-
whelms both common sense and spiritual
convictions. That's why there are objec-
tive rules to follow.

But rules by themselves will not cause

right behavior. You must first choose to evaluate a borrowing decision relative to these rules. Then you have to act on the basis of that evaluation, which is the most difficult part of the process, because it may mean not having something you really want. On the other hand, choosing to act the way you believe you should will ultimately create a tremendous sense of satisfaction. Self-esteem goes up as you make right decisions.

Weighing today's desires against future benefits is a classic psychological definition of maturity. These rules, then, will help you act maturely.

Rule 1: Common Sense
This rule can be stated as follows: *For borrowing to make sense, the economic return must be greater than the economic cost.* To state it another way, when money

is borrowed, the thing it was borrowed to purchase should either grow in value or pay an economic return greater than the cost of borrowing. I call this a common-sense rule because it makes no sense whatsoever to break it.

Looking at this rule in reverse, it makes no sense at all to borrow money if it's going to cost you more to borrow than what you're going to get in the way of an economic return. That return can be twofold. The thing purchased can grow in value, such as a home, or it can pay a return, such as a stock that pays dividends.

To ignore this rule is to say, in effect, that you're willing to borrow money and pay 12 percent interest in order to deposit it in a savings account earning 5 percent interest. Yet every day, many people agree to rent money at a much higher cost than they can ever expect to receive in the way of an economic return. (Things like clothes and restaurant meals, of course, provide no financial return at all.)

Rule 2: A Guaranteed Way to Repay

If you borrow money to buy a home, and the lender is willing to take back the home as full payment of the debt in the event you're unable to pay, you have a guaranteed way to repay the debt. You're not presuming the continuation of favorable economic conditions.

Another example of consistency with this rule is the use of a credit card for convenience's sake. When I use my credit card to pay for some dry cleaning, I do this knowing the money is already in the bank to pay for the service. Using a card this way, strictly for convenience with the money in the bank, does not presume upon the future.

There are only three sources from which to repay borrowed money:

1. Income earned from sources other than that for which the money was borrowed.
2. The sale of whatever the money was borrowed for.
3. The sale or liquidation of some other asset, such as a certificate of deposit or savings account.

The reliability of those sources of repayment depends on many factors. Only you, as the potential borrower, can make that evaluation.

Rule 3: Peace of Heart and Mind

To determine whether you satisfy rule 3, you must ask yourself:

1. Why am I doing what I'm doing?
2. Does what I'm doing violate any ethical or spiritual principle?

3. Do I have peace in my heart or spirit?
4. Do I have peace of mind when envisioning doing what I'm doing?

The first question gets at motives. Is the reason for borrowing to get rich quick, to avoid working, to satisfy a want, to give an appearance other than the truth, to meet a need, or to attain some other desire?

This is a penetrating question to have to ask yourself. If you can become disciplined enough to ask it and answer honestly before every borrowing decision, at the very least it will cause you to delay making impulsive decisions. In most cases, it will keep you from borrowing for the wrong reasons. If you're unwilling even to ask yourself the question, the chances are pretty good your motives aren't right.

Another way to check your motives is

to explain to your spouse or a good friend why you're doing what you're doing. Most of us are masters at deceiving ourselves so we can justify what we want to do. But when we have to explain our motives to someone else and it's unpleasant or uncomfortable, or if the borrowing "just doesn't sound right" to that person, our motives are most likely wrong.

After answering the first question, you almost always know the answer to the second. If the motive is wrong—greed, lack of discipline, lack of contentment— you know you're violating a spiritual principle.

To illustrate the application of this rule, suppose a man could afford to pay $25,000 cash for a car, enough to buy a moderately priced new car or a nice used one. On the other hand, if he adds $15,000 of debt to this amount, he could drive a new luxury car. He may even be able to "afford" the payments on this luxury car. By asking himself, *Why am I considering going into debt to buy the luxury car?* he's challenging himself to examine his motives.

Closely related to peace of heart is peace of mind. I would separate the two this way: The mind is the intellectual evaluation, whereas the heart is the spiritual and emotional evaluation. Applying this to a borrowing decision, you should ask yourself, *Am I free from confusion about this? Do I have clear thinking and a solid conviction that this is the right decision?*

The questions related to this rule are not all-inclusive. They're meant to get you to examine your motives.

Rule 4: Unity

I don't understand it, but I know that women have an intuitive sense about financial decisions that men usually don't. I also don't know why my wife can see things clearly that I can't seem to see at all. But I do know that when I've listened to her out of respect for her insight—and even gone against what I felt to be right— I have avoided problem situations.

The rule of unity applies to all of a family's financial decisions—investments as well as borrowing. Specifically regarding investing, I have two rules for the person who wants to make an investment: (1) If you can't explain it to your spouse, don't do it. (2) Even if you can explain it and your spouse understands, if your spouse doesn't feel good about it, don't do it.

A commitment to unity between marriage partners (or, in the case of a single person, with an accountability partner) will help avoid most debt problems. But because accountability and unity go against our natures, this is the rule most often violated. Many men even consider it unreasonable. Their comment to me is, "You don't know my wife" or "You don't live with my wife." And, of course, they're right: I don't understand their wives. I don't understand my own wife many times!

When I entered into marriage, however, I implicitly agreed that it was no longer "her way" or "my way" but now "our way." And a debt decision that I make can have tremendous impact not only on her sense of security but also on her *real* security. Thus, I am obligated morally and ethically to make her a part of that decision.

I would encourage you to reread the rules so they become ingrained in your thought life to the point that you aren't even tempted to make a foolish debt decision. Let me say again, however, that I'm not asserting that borrowing money is always wrong. Only the failure to repay is wrong. Following these rules will help you live with a great deal of inner peace, as well as peace within your family.

ͻ ͻ ͻ

Let me give you one final piece of advice. Making good financial decisions will, at times, require accepting the fact that you cannot have everything you want. Deciding that you will do whatever it takes to escape an ocean of debt may result in extreme sacrifice by you and your family. It may mean giving up a vacation, a car, a business opportunity, clothes, or something else you desperately want.

But debt is an illusion promising "something for nothing," when the reality is that you *can't* have something for nothing.

The positive side of the decision to get out of debt and stay out of debt is that you are no longer putting yourself in a position that in the future could risk everything—your reputation, your family, and all you've accumulated financially.

By reading this book, you've taken the first step. You *can* get out of debt. You *can* formulate a healthy financial perspective and make better decisions for you and your family. It takes time and effort, but the peace that comes from living with financial freedom is worth it.

Notes

1. Jon Birger, "Should You Cash Out While You Can?" *Money,* August 1, 2005, http://money .cnn.com/magazines/moneymag/money mag_archive/2005/08/01/8267026/index.htm.
2. Eric Schurenberg, "Getting on Top of Your Debt," *Money,* April 1, 1987, http://money .cnn.com.com/magazines/moneymag/money mag_archive/1987/04/01/83806/index.htm.
3. Kathy Chu, "Spending Contributes to Inability to Save," *USA Today,* May 22, 2006, http:// www.usatoday.com/money/perfi/basics/ 2006-05-22-mayberrys-profile_x.htm.

Resources

Blue, Ron. *Splitting Heirs*. Chicago: Northfield Publishing, 2004.

Blue, Ron. *Taming the Money Monster*. Carol Stream, Ill.: Focus on the Family/Tyndale House Publishers, 1993.

Blue, Ron, and Jeremy White. *The New Master Your Money*. Chicago: Moody Publishers, 2004.

Blue, Ron, Judy Blue, and Jeremy White. *Your Kids Can Master Their Money*. Carol Stream, Ill.: Focus on the Family/Tyndale House Publishers, 2006.

Burkett, Larry, and Ron Blue. *The Burkett and Blue Definitive Guide to Securing Wealth to Last*. Nashville, Tenn.: Broadman and Holman Publishers, 2003.

Burkett, Larry, and Ron Blue. *Your Money After the Big 5-0*. Nashville, Tenn.: Broadman and Holman Publishers, 2007.

Dr. Bill Maier is Focus on the Family's vice president and psychologist in residence. Dr. Maier received his master's and doctoral degrees from the Rosemead School of Psychology at Biola University in La Mirada, California. A child and family psychologist, Dr. Maier hosts the national television feature *Focus on Your Family with Dr. Bill Maier,* and the national *Weekend Magazine* and *Family Minute with Dr. Bill Maier* radio programs. In addition, Dr. Maier is a media spokes-person for Focus on the Family on a variety of family-related issues. He and his wife, Lisa, have been married for more than seven years and have three children.

ɔ ɔ ɔ

Ron Blue has been a financial planner and consultant for over 40 years. He received his master's degree in business administration from Indiana University. Ron has appeared on numerous radio and television programs, including *Focus on the Family, Family News in Focus, The 700 Club, Prime Time America,* and *Moody Radio Open Line.* He has authored over 17 books on personal finance, including the best-selling *Master Your Money* and *Your Kids Can Master Their Money.* Ron is a regular contributor to several national Christian magazines. He and his wife, Judy, live in Atlanta. They have five children and nine grandchildren.

FOCUS ON THE FAMILY®

Welcome to the family!

Whether you purchased this book, borrowed it, or received it as a gift, we're glad you're reading it. It's just one of the many helpful, encouraging, and biblically based resources produced by Focus on the Family for people in all stages of life.

Focus began in 1977 with the vision of one man, Dr. James Dobson, a licensed psychologist and author of numerous best-selling books on marriage, parenting, and family. Alarmed by the societal, political, and economic pressures that were threatening the existence of the American family, Dr. Dobson founded Focus on the Family with one employee and a once-a-week radio broadcast aired on 36 stations.

Now an international organization reaching millions of people daily, Focus on the Family is dedicated to preserving values and strengthening and encouraging families through the life-changing message of Jesus Christ.

Focus on the Family Magazines

These faith-building, character-developing publications address the interests, issues, concerns, and challenges faced by every member of your family from preschool through the senior years.

Focus on the Family **Citizen®** U.S. news issues	Focus on the Family **Clubhouse Jr.™** Ages 4 to 8	Focus on the Family **Clubhouse™** Ages 8 to 12	**Breakaway®** Teen guys	**Brio®** Teen girls 12 to 16	**Brio & Beyond®** Teen girls 16 to 19	**Plugged In®** Reviews movies, music, TV

FOR MORE INFORMATION

Online:
Log on to www.family.org
In Canada, log on to
www.focusonthefamily.ca

Phone:
Call toll free: (800) A-FAMILY
In Canada, call toll free:
(800) 661-9800

More Great Resources
from Focus on the Family®

Your Kids Can Master Their Money:
Fun Ways to Help Them Learn How
by Ron and Judy Blue & Jeremy White
Written by financial advisors Ron and Judy Blue
along with Jeremy White, this book shows children how creatively using and saving money can
be fun—and rewarding. It's an investment in your
children's outlook on finances that will have great
payoffs in their adult lives.

Help! My Adult Child Won't Leave Home
by Stephen Bly
Dr. Bill Maier, General Editor
While a parent's role changes with age and circumstances, we remain parents. Whether a child
is an adult and should be ready to leave home, or
they move back home for a season, here's advice
on how to show your love in a healthy way.

Help! Someone I Know Has a Problem
with Porn
by Jim Vigorito, Ph.D.
Dr. Bill Maier, General Editor
Does someone you know have a problem with
porn? Today's technologies have opened even more
venues for pornography access. You may know
someone who is caught in the porn trap. This
book offers practical advice on several key topics.

FOR MORE INFORMATION

Online:
Log on to www.family.org
In Canada, log on to www.focusonthefamily.ca.

Phone:
Call toll free: (800) A-FAMILY
In Canada, call toll free: (800) 661-9800.

Focus
on the Family®

BP06XP1